HOW TO PLAY GIRLS'
SOFTBALL

MESSNER BOOKS BY ARNOLD MADISON

How To Play Girls' Softball
Don't Be a Victim
   Protect Yourself and Your Belongings
Smoking and You
Drugs and You

HOW TO PLAY GIRLS' SOFTBALL

by Arnold Madison

Illustrated with photographs
by Kevin Shaw

Julian Messner

New York

JULIAN MESSNER and colophon are trademarks of
Simon & Schuster.
Third printing, 1983
Manufactured in the United States of America

Design by Philip Jaget

Library of Congress Cataloging in Publication Data

Madison, Arnold.
    How to play girls' softball.

    Includes index.
    SUMMARY: Discusses history, equipment, clothing,
rules, batting, playing the various positions,
skills and techniques, throwing, and health.
    1.   Softball for women—Juvenile literature.
[1. Softball]   I. Title.
GV881.3.M33   796.357'8   81-479
ISBN 0-671-33051-9   AACR1

ACKNOWLEDGMENTS

The author and photographer wish to thank Mrs. Marguerite Lewis for her assistance with this book. A special thank you is due the Bethlehem Tomboys Softball League of Delmar, New York. The Union National Bank team managed by William Westerhouse and coached by Phil DeGaetano and John Kolonoski were especially giving of their time and talents to help produce the photographs for this book. And, of course, the players themselves deserve our gratitude: Pamela Cashin, Laura DeGaetano, Cynthia Ferrari, Jennifer Fritts, Julie Kolonoski, D'arcy LeMaitre, Vicki Manion, Donna McAndrews, Karen O'Keeffe, Lissa Potter, Kirsten Wehmann, Doranne Westerhouse, Kelly Westerhouse, and Samantha Wood.

CONTENTS

HOW TO PLAY GIRLS'
SOFTBALL

Chapter 1.

Cinderella at Bat

The Arizona sun blazed in a blue sky as Lisa Diaz wiped the sweat from her forehead and stared at the pitcher. The count was three balls and two strikes. Lisa knew the next pitch had to be a strike. Wiping her palms on her jeans, she gripped the bat so it felt balanced and comfortable in her hands. She tapped the far outside of the plate once, twice, with the bat and then settled into her favorite hitting position.

The pitcher wound up and delivered. Lisa eyed the ball as it sailed in a straight, unwavering line. A moment more . . . now!

The bat swished through the hot air.

"Three strikes and out!" called the umpire.

Lisa angrily kicked the dusty earth. That would be the last time she would be a sucker for a knuckle-ball pitch. Wait until the next game.

Meanwhile, over 2,000 miles away, Bettina Washington stood on third base. The breeze coming from the Adirondack Mountains in the distance fanned her face. But despite the coolness, anxiety made her feel flushed. If only her teammate could get a hit. It was the seventh inning; the score was tied.

As the ball left the pitcher's hand, Bettina edged a few steps toward home plate. The resounding crack as the bat struck the ball sent shivers of excitement through her. Immediately, she took off for home. There was no need to watch the ball which had gone over the outfielders' heads. Her foot tagged the plate,

and her teammates slapped her on the back in congratulations. She watched as the batter rounded second and aimed for third. Outfielders were still scrambling for the ball. Bettina grinned as her teammate slowly walked the last few steps to home plate.

What do Lisa Diaz and Bettina Washington have in common? They are members of two softball teams.

Lisa's team is from Mesa, Arizona, which, because it has so

many softball teams, is often regarded as the softball capital of the United States. Bettina is a softball Little League Player—one of about 153,000 girls who form thousands of softball teams in every state. Her league is sometimes called the Cinderella League.

If someone from another country had been watching either game, that person might have thought it was a game of baseball, since baseball is better known because it is often broadcast on television. The uniforms, protective equipment, playing field, gloves, action on the field, and most of the expressions or terms are the same or similar to those in baseball.

Actually, Lisa was playing a particular form of softball known as *slow-pitch softball*, while Bettina was playing *fast-pitch softball*. Although fast-pitch is popular among professional softball players and organized amateur teams and leagues, it is not the most popular form of softball. That title belongs to slow-pitch softball. There are other types of softball besides these, but fast-pitch and slow-pitch are the two main ones.

The outstanding features of any form of softball are pitching the ball underhand and the use of a larger ball.

Slow-pitch has rules that make it just right for sandlot playing and having fun. It is a hitter's game and, as everyone knows, there is nothing more satisfying than being able to slam the ball and have fielders running like blazes to catch it.

Who Can Play Softball?

It makes little difference who plays the game—male or female. You can be an amateur or professional, and play at any age. There are tournaments, leagues, and teams to fit your ability. And there is a Hall of Fame honoring the players of the past. It is located in Oklahoma City, Oklahoma.

How Softball Started

The first softball game was played indoors between a group of former Harvard and Yale students at a boat club near the shores of Lake Michigan, in Chicago, in 1887. That's only a year after the beginning of baseball's National League, the oldest in major league baseball.

No one knows how it happened, but according to one historian, softball next appeared in Minneapolis, Minnesota, eight years later. A certain Lieutenant Lewis Rober of Fire Company Number 11 organized a game which he called Kitten Ball. Since firemen are on call 24 hours a day, they were looking for something to do to pass their time while waiting for an alarm.

Rober made it into an outdoor game, playing it in a vacant lot next to the firehouse. He wrote a set of rules, and other fire companies promptly challenged Fire Company 11 to play Kitten Ball.

The next year, Rober was transferred to another company, where he organized a team. Soon there were teams all over Minneapolis, and the Kitten Ball fever spread to nearby St. Paul. By 1900, there was a league, made up of teams like the Kittens, the Rats, and the Whales. Sometimes as many as several thousand people came to see the games.

By 1922, the name Kitten Ball had been dropped, and for a time the game was called Mush Ball or Diamond Ball. Later it was even called Pumpkin Ball, Big Ball, and other names.

The name *softball* came along in 1926. Six years later, there were 40 teams in six states attending a national championship tournament in Minneapolis.

In 1933, the Amateur Softball Association (ASA) was founded. In that year, the Hearst newspaper chain sponsored a nationwide softball tournament to be played at the Chicago

World's Fair. Over 70,000 people watched those championship games.

Leo Fischer, a sportswriter, who was the main organizer of the Chicago World's Fair Tournament, set up the rules committee of ASA and became first president of ASA. During the next few years, the Hearst newspaper chain continued to support amateur softball.

Throughout its growth, softball has been the place where people could go to have fun as amateur ballplayers. There are a lot of experts in the game who say that anyone who gets serious about softball should choose another sport.

Chapter 2.

Uniforms and Equipment

Although softball is a game of fun, to be played mostly in vacant lots or at the playground, sooner or later, you're going to consider playing it as an amateur. You will then go on to belong to an organized team and even a league.

Girls' softball teams can either be sponsored by a local business organization, or it can be part of the school sports program or the Little League. If you are playing on any such team, you will be given a uniform. In some cases you will even receive gloves and bats to be used during the games. However, if you and your friends have organized informal teams, you will have to get your own uniforms and equipment.

However, the lack of a uniform should not prevent anyone from getting out on the field and playing the game.

The Uniform

The official uniform of softball is quite similar to that of baseball. Being female is not going to make much difference, but you should not wear any jewelry.

The most important thing is that your uniform should give you freedom of movement. If any piece of clothing is too tight, get rid of it and find one that is the next larger size. Don't wear tight jeans just because you look well in them. They might prevent you from catching a fly ball or scooping up a grounder.

A softball uniform can be a T-shirt, jeans, and sneakers such as the pitcher is wearing.

The various parts of your uniform should provide protection. For example, many players prefer to wear a loose-fitting, long-sleeved sweatshirt to keep their arms warm. This is especially important for pitchers. If the game is played on a cloudy, wind-swept day or early evening, perspiration will evaporate quickly. A pitcher might suffer from the tightening muscles in her arm. It will be sore and painful when she pitches. A long-sleeved sweat-shirt will keep those muscles warm and loose.

Over the sweatshirt, some girls prefer to wear a short-sleeved T-shirt. It's not meant to give warmth, but it's a good idea for the whole team to wear the same color so you can all be recognized as being on the same team.

Shorts that do not bind are excellent for softball. Think about the rules of the game before deciding whether to wear shorts or jeans. If sliding is permitted, then shorts are the worst possible clothing to wear. Instead, wear long, loose-fitting jeans which will withstand the rough gravel as you slide into base or home plate. Jeans will hide legs or thighs that have been taped and they will keep elastic bandages from coming loose.

On your feet, you will need thick high stockings to help prevent scrapes around the ankles. Many players recommend that two pairs of stockings be worn. This will help stop blisters from forming. Before putting on your stockings, sprinkle a fungicide-type foot powder, such as Desetin or Desenex, over your feet. If you apply the powder before and after a game, you cut down the chances of getting the infection known as athlete's foot.

Playing shoes need good traction. A new pair of sneakers with good heels and soles will do the trick. If you want softball shoes that have canvas or leather uppers and rubber cleats, you can get them at a sports shop. The cleats may be either hard or soft rub-ber. Although it isn't necessary, some players prefer shoes with metal spikes. These are legal as long as the spikes do not extend more than three-fourths of an inch from the heel or sole. However, rounded metal spikes are illegal.

For a game of informal softball, a pair of sneakers with deep treads and soles will do.

As for hats, the catcher must wear a baseball cap with a brim. The purpose is to prevent the sun from causing her to lose sight of the ball. In fact, all players should wear caps for the same reason.

Any jewelry such as bracelets, watches, or neck chains should be removed. Even rings are best taken off to prevent injury while batting or catching a ball. A ring is especially dangerous if the finger is injured and then becomes swollen. The doctor might have to cut the ring off to insure the flow of blood.

Bats

The equipment in a softball game is the bat, ball, and glove or mitt. Certain rules apply to these items.

The rules say that the bat may be constructed from various materials: plastic, bamboo, wood, or metal. A metal bat, however, should have a smooth surface, with no dangerous edges or sharp spots such as rivets, pins, or fasteners. A metal bat with a wooden handle is not allowed because the wood can snap or splinter.

The softball bat is shorter and lighter than a baseball bat. Most players prefer a bat made of wood. They are cheaper than metal ones.

All bats should have safety grip material of either cork or tape on the handle. This protective covering should not be less than ten inches long, or extend more than 15 inches from the small end of the bat.

This wooden bat has tape on the handle.

Selecting a bat has little to do with your size, height, or weight. You should choose one that is comfortable in your hands. As for length, no bat can be longer than 34 inches.

When not in use, bats should always be in a rack. Players can be seriously injured by stumbling over a bat on the ground.

The Softball

It's not really soft. Ask anyone who gets hit with one. It is as hard as a baseball. An official softball is made of sections of horsehide, cowhide, or a synthetic material and is filled with either long-fiber kapok or a mixture of cork and rubber.

Three different sizes are used, depending upon which type of game is being played. The ball most often used has a circumference of between $11^7/_8$ inches and $12^1/_4$ inches. Nevertheless, this ball is generally called the 12-inch ball. It should weigh between $6^1/_4$ and 7 ounces. This size ball is used in slow-pitch, fast-pitch, and modified fast-pitch softball.

An official softball is made of sections of horsehide, cowhide, or a synthetic material.

A 16-inch ball is used, too, but its use makes the game come under "official 16-inch rules." They cannot be given in full here, but they include the rule that a 16-inch ball game must be played on a diamond that is ten feet shorter between bases than in slow-pitch and fast-pitch games played by females. The pitching distance for both men and women is 38 feet. This is a shorter pitching distance than in any other form of softball.

In slow-pitch softball, a 14-inch ball is still sometimes used, but it is losing popularity. However, there are no official rules against its use.

In games that start with one size of ball, no switch to any other size is allowed. That's because different rules apply to each size.

Glove or Mitt

The last important piece of equipment is the leather glove or mitt that you will use on the field. Mitts are worn only by the first baseperson and catcher. All other players wear gloves.

A glove has individual fingers as well as an indentation or pocket in the palm. A mitt has a thumb slot and a larger section for the other fingers. Both gloves and mitts may have lacing or webbing between the thumb and forefinger.

Colors and decorations of gloves and mitts are strictly regulated. For instance, the pitcher's glove has to be a single color but neither white or gray. The reason for this is that players would not be able to see if the pitcher held the ball in her glove. This would give her an unfair advantage. She would be able to surprise players on base, and pick them off too easily when they start to lead off the base. Other players, however, may have multi-colored gloves, but even these cannot have designs of white or gray circles which might be mistaken as a ball.

A glove, made of leather, has individual fingers and lacing or webbing between the thumb and forefinger.

Once you have enjoyed several games of softball and have really become caught up in the sport, you may decide to buy your own glove. Don't rush into making this purchase. First, try out different gloves or mitts so you will know the one that feels best for you. Perhaps you might take an experienced softball player with you to the sports shop. He or she can give you some advice.

When you take the brand new glove or mitt home, you will have to condition it before playing with it. There are no official rules about how to prepare your glove, but be sure you do so. Conditioning will prolong the glove's usefulness. Also, you want to become accustomed to the mitt or glove as quickly as possible so you can use it.

The conditioning process means first massaging oil or another leather softener into the glove. Many players prefer Neat's-foot oil, but check with the sports shop where you bought your glove. Work this oil or softener into the entire glove, especially the seams. It acts as a protective coating to ward off moisture, dust, and perspiration that may punish the leather during a game. One application will not be enough. Repeat the treatment after each game until the glove is fully broken-in.

Some girls like to begin shaping the glove pocket at home, instead of breaking it in on the field. This will make catching easier. The procedure is slow but it works. While wearing the glove on the hand, repeatedly throw the ball into the glove. Be sure to catch the ball each time where you would normally grab a softball during a game.

Another, even more professional, way to break in a glove is to put a ball in the pocket and tie the glove tightly around it. Leave it overnight. Do this each night after applying the oil.

If you become bored with the glove-shaping, you might help

the process along by pounding a ball into the pocket for a half-hour at a time for a few days. Of course, you could also round up a few friends and have practice catch sessions. Not only would you be improving your throwing and catching skills, but you would be conditioning the glove. During the same break-in period, keep working Neat's-foot oil or a softener into the glove so the leather will respond more quickly to the shaping process.

At the end of the softball season, gloves and mitts should be oiled and stored with a ball or wad of paper stuffed in the pocket.

Now—you have your uniform and equipment. The time has come for you to join your team and begin developing those skills that will make you an outstanding player.

Chapter 3.

How to Play Softball

It is not necessary to know all the rules of softball unless you are planning to be a professional or semi-professional player. You will need to learn only those rules that apply to the kind of game you want to become skilled at.

If you don't know which type of game you would like best, then a quick reading of the rules might help you decide. The principal games are: slow-pitch, fast-pitch, modified fast-pitch, and 16-inch ball. However, reading the rules will probably not be enough. Playing or watching the different types of games would be better. You can also get an official guide to the rules of all the games. It's not very expensive, either. Write to:

Amateur Softball Association of America
Box 1143
Oklahoma City, OK 73136

Players

Each fast-pitch softball team must have nine players on the field: pitcher, catcher, first baseperson, second baseperson, shortstop, third baseperson, right fielder, center fielder, and left fielder. Each player can change her position at any time during the game. Substitute players may be used during a game. However, once a player is removed, she may not return. The substitute player hits in her place in the batting order.

In slow-pitch softball, a tenth player is added. She is the short-fielder. In some teams she is called a "rover," because her position may be anywhere in the outfield.

The Playing Field

A fast-pitch softball game is played on a field whose edge or fence is 225 feet from home plate. The slow-pitch game field measures 250 feet from home plate.

In both types of fields, there are foul lines between home plate and third base on the left, and between home plate and first base on the right. These lines, which extend into the outfield, are marked in white. Any ball that lands beyond these lines is out of play, unless caught by a fielder on the fly.

The pitcher's plate is 40 feet from home plate in fast-pitch, and 46 feet away in slow-pitch. There is a circle around the pitcher's plate which limits where the pitcher can stand.

The batter's box is three feet wide and seven feet long. It is the same in all the games, but is marked off on both sides of the plate for left- and right-handed batters. There is an on deck circle on each side of home plate for the next batter.

The area between bases for both fast-pitch and slow-pitch games measures 60 feet. In the popular 16-inch ball game, the distance between bases is only 50 feet and the pitching distance is reduced to 38 feet.

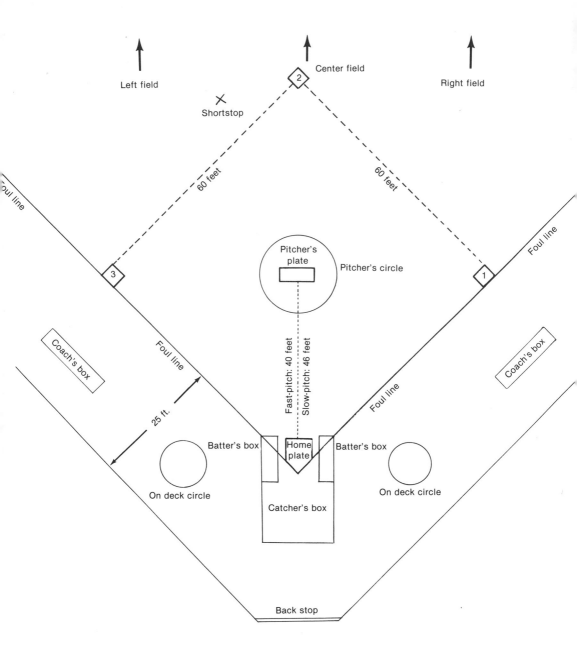

Girls' Softball Diamond.

Umpires

There are one or more umpires, but no umpire can be connected with the game in any way other than as an umpire. If there are two, one of them enforces and interprets the rules and settles all disputes from behind home plate, while the other does the same from a position on the field. Neither umpire is allowed to overrule the other.

If the game is fast-pitch, the home plate umpire must wear a body guard and mask. Neither is required in slow-pitch, but is recommended.

The umpire in the field declares the runner out.

The plate umpire stays immediately behind the catcher to be in the best possible position to judge the ball and the batter.

The Game

The home team bats last in each inning. However, if the game is played on a neutral field, a home team is decided by the toss of a coin. A fast-pitch softball game is played in seven innings. The slow-pitch game lasts nine innings.

If the home team is leading by the second half of the last inning, that second half is not played. Should the game be tied at the end of either seven or nine innings, the teams continue to play until one side has scored more runs at the end of a complete inning.

At times, a game may be called due to darkness, weather, or injuries. Under these circumstances, the umpire makes the decision to end the game. If five or more innings have been completed, the game is considered an official one. The umpire may also rule that a team has forfeited a game if it fails to appear.

Pitching Rules

The main differences between slow-pitch softball and fast-pitch softball is in the way the ball is thrown at the batter and the speed it has. In slow-pitch, the ball must arch upward at least three feet above the pitcher's hand at the point where she releases the ball. However, it must never arch higher than 12 feet off the ground.

This arching throw helps the ball to come in more slowly than in fast-pitch softball. The umpire decides on the top speed of a ball in slow-pitch and may warn a pitcher if she throws the ball too fast.

Slow-pitch gives the batter more chances to hit the ball. Because more balls are hit, there is more action on the field and higher scores. As a result, slow-pitch is the favorite game of about 80 percent of those who play softball.

A game begins with the umpire's announcement to "Play ball." The players are in position and the first batter steps into the batter's box.

In fast-pitch, the pitcher stands with her feet firmly on the ground and touching the pitcher's plate. In a slow-pitch game, she must have one or both feet on the ground and touching the pitcher's plate.

She holds the ball in front of her body for not less than one second nor for more than 20. In fast-pitch, the pitch officially begins as soon as the pitcher takes one hand off the ball. In slow-pitch, the game starts when she goes into her wind-up motion.

Throwing the ball underhand, she completes the pitch when she advances one step toward the batter and releases the ball. The pitcher may use any wind-up she chooses, so long as the movements are immediately followed by delivering the ball to the batter. She is not allowed to use a rocker action or make more than one revolution of her arm while delivering the pitch.

A slow-pitch pitcher should take a few steps backward after the ball leaves her hand since batters often are able to slam the ball straight at her. Most pitchers learn to jump backward automatically.

The pitcher.

A pitch is illegal if the pitcher drops the ball, rolls it, or bounces it in order to prevent the batter from striking it or if she uses tape or any other substance on the ball. Under these circumstances, a ball is called on the batter and the runners can advance one base.

Rules for Strikes and Fouls

In both types of games, if the batter swings and misses a pitch, a strike is called. A foul ball is declared when the ball is hit but lands outside the foul lines. The foul is an out if caught on the fly. If not caught, it is a strike, unless there are already two strikes on the batter, just as in baseball.

A foul tip is a hit ball which lands directly in the catcher's hands and is held by her. A foul tip will be considered a strike no matter how many strikes have been called against the batter. The batter is ruled out whenever a fly ball is caught in fair or foul territory.

Chapter 4.

Hitting and Running: The Basic Offensive Skills

The skills that you'll need to add to your team's score are: batting, running, and sliding. Players should practice these skills off the playing field as well as during regular team practice sessions. Batting can be strengthened while working out with one or more players. Running and sliding can be perfected in the schoolyard, backyard, or on an empty ball field.

On a fast-pitch softball team, more practice is needed in batting and running, while on a slow-pitch team, the most important skills are the opposite—the defensive skills, which will be dealt with later in this chapter. They are pitching and catching. See Chapter 6 for a discussion of the more advanced offensive skills.

Batting

The first thing to develop is your *stance*. This word means how you stand at home plate while preparing to hit the ball, but that's not all. Stance also takes into consideration placement of feet, arms, and body.

To begin with, how far should you stand from the plate?

There is a general rule. Stand at home plate, bend at the

The correct batting stance.

waist, and touch the tip of the bat to the outside corner of the plate. Be sure to hold the bat with a normal grip. The tip should rest comfortably without straining any portion of your body.

To have a good stance, stand opposite the plate with your legs spaced about shoulder-width apart. Your feet should be parallel. This is called an "open stance." Your body is facing the plate, but your shoulder on the pitcher's side and your head are facing the pitcher. Relax your knees and crouch slightly.

The word relax is an important one. Normally, in a game, you will have a tendency to be tense while awaiting the pitch. You must learn to be at ease. Relax your hips. Hold the bat so your hands are about level with your shoulder, and the bat is behind your head, but not resting on your shoulder.

At first, you may feel awkward holding your elbows away from your body, but this is absolutely necessary. If your elbows are too close, you will jam yourself and interfere with your swing. Keep your forward arm horizontal with the ground. By dropping your back arm just a bit, you will add more power to the swing.

Once you have this stance, you can then consider your grip on the bat. You have selected a bat that was best for your height, weight, and strength. It is one that feels balanced and easy to swing. If it has the weight you feel good with, it will add force to your swing.

There are three possible grips: long, medium, and short or choke. Whatever grip you prefer, hold the bat with one hand on top of the other, close together, and your fingers and thumbs wrapped around the handle. For right-handed players, the right hand is placed on top. Left-handed batters set the left hand above the right hand.

Now let's examine each of the three grips.

The *long grip* is used for a long swing—to hit the ball hard and for a long distance. It is a home run grip. Your hands should grasp the bat as close to the bottom of the knob as possible.

The *medium grip* is the most popular among softball players. Not only does the bat feel quite comfortable, but it allows the player to hit the ball fairly hard. The batter is also able to direct the ball toward a particular area of the field. To get this grip, slide your hands about one to two inches above the knob end of the bat.

The *choke grip* will allow the batter to hit the ball toward any spot in the outfield. This grip works best against fast pitches. Your hands grip the bat about three to four inches above the knob. Remember, you can't get much distance on the ball with this grip.

The long grip.

The medium grip.

A batter needs a lot of concentration. The only thing she should feel is the bat in her hands. Ignore voices around you and the sound of the crowd. Shut out everything except the pitcher and the ball she will be throwing. Remember—in the fast-pitch game, the ball takes only from one-third to one-half second to travel from the pitcher to the batter. You will need to decide quickly how, when, or if to hit that rapidly moving sphere. This is why batting practice is so important in a fast-pitch game.

Veteran players warn rookies to fight off any doubts: just say "I'm going to hit that ball." Save your doubts for later. This is known as "psyching yourself up," and, according to experienced athletes, it will work if you give it a chance.

The short or choke grip.

Now let's see what happens. The pitcher winds up and throws the ball. As it leaves her hand, you should shift your weight to the rear foot. At the same time, move the other foot forward a bit and point your toes at the pitcher. During the moment of shifting weight, your hips and shoulders will shift slightly away from the pitcher as your body pivots back. You are ready!

Keep your eye on the ball. As the moment of impact arrives, start your swing, snapping your wrists forward. At the same time, push hard against the ground with the inside of the back foot. Then step forward with the front foot, digging it into the ground so that this leg will be braced for the instant the bat strikes the ball. Roll your wrists slightly, and continue with your arms in the follow-through of the swing. Even though your weight is completely on the front leg, your back foot keeps contact with the ground so you don't lose your balance.

Be sure your hips and shoulders remain horizontal. By doing this, the bat will strike the ball in front of your body.

If you swing the bat upward—what is called an "upper cut" —you will hit a fly ball that the outfielder can easily catch for an out, unless you hit it for a home run.

If you swing downward, a grounder will result. Some players suggest that a batter always swing downward and never upward. Experience will tell you when either is called for.

Most players prefer the level swing. This can produce either a hard-hit ground ball or a powerful line drive. Such hits are not always stopped, so that the batter may get at least one base while other teammates already on base may be able to advance or even reach home plate to score a run.

In the slow-pitch game, the batter has more time to judge the speed and position of the ball. She may, if she is good or lucky, zap the ball hard and into a spot where there are no fielders. Or, if she's taken an upper cut, the ball may zoom over the fence for a home run.

Bunting

In the fast-pitch game, a form of batting called *bunting* can be used to advance runners on base. It is not allowed in the slow-pitch game. When you bunt, you do not swing the bat at all. Just let the bat make contact with the ball so that the ball loses force. By skillful bunting, you can "place" the ball about ten to twenty feet from the plate and as close to a base line as possible.

There are two reasons for doing this. First, by bunting, you can pull the first baseperson, the pitcher, or even the third baseperson toward home plate. You run to first base, and the ball is thrown there to tag you out. Meanwhile, the runner who was on first is now safely on second. You have "bunted" her to second base while "sacrificing" yourself in order to do it.

The *sacrifice bunt* makes more sense if your team is desperately in need of only one run to tie or win. You get a base runner to second so that if the next batter gets a hit, there is a good chance that the player on second can get home. If that happens—and it often does—it would mean that your bunt was the hit that set up the winning or tying run.

The second reason is one of surprise—to the opposing team. Suppose that the infielders are playing far back. A bunt is not expected when you see this. If you do bunt, it would cause them to run in, leaving their positions open. Also, the distance they have to scramble in order to grab the ball is great. By bunting, you may gain a little extra time to reach first base.

An experienced softball player explained why she preferred to bunt when the circumstances were right. Generally, the pitcher is the person who fields a bunted ball. Softball pitchers, in this girl's opinion, are poor overhand throwers. They rely so frequently on underhand pitches that their skill and aim with an overhand throw is weak. Often the pitcher will throw wide of first base, pulling the baseperson off the bag.

Whatever the reason for bunting, try not to give away that you're going to do it. It's a technique that should be executed at the last minute.

When you're ready, turn and face the pitcher squarely and bring your rear foot forward. Hold the bat with two hands in a horizontal position in front of you with the hitting end extended beyond your body.

Slide your top hand to just below the bat's trademark. This

Holding the bat to bunt.

hand should be upside down, so that the fingers seem to be pinching the bat. Keep those fingers off the side of the bat that will be hitting the ball. Also, be sure your hand is below the hitting area. Bunting a ball with your fingers can be very painful and most likely will result in an out for your side.

The best pitches to bunt are those that are low. High inside pitches are very difficult to hit because you will have to bring the bat up rather than down. This may allow the pitcher to run in and catch the fly ball.

When the ball hits the bat, you should angle the ball downward and to the right, center, or left. Most bunts are aimed toward the first or third baseperson. The bunt may cause confusion for a moment between the baseperson and the pitcher about who should field the bunt. Every second you can gain to reach first base is valuable.

A *drag bunt* is one that is hit as close to the base line as possible. The catcher is then forced to move forward to field the ball, but then she has a difficult throw to execute. You, the runner, are in a direct line between catcher and first baseperson. The catcher has to be extremely careful not to hit you with the thrown ball.

Whether you hit a regular bunt or a drag bunt, you begin running *as* you bunt the ball. This gives you a head start until the catcher realizes she must move in to grab the ball. You should then run past the bunted ball before the catcher has had a chance to grab it and throw to the first baseperson.

Another technique related to bunting is *fake bunting*. As the name implies, you start to bunt but do not complete it—that is, you don't make contact with the ball. Instead, with the first pitch, you slip into a bunting position but pull back as soon as the ball leaves the pitcher's hand.

This action alerts the infielders. They may move in close to be ready if you do bunt the next pitch. Then, do it again with the next pitch. In this bunt position, you quickly go back to your hitting stance and swing hard. If you aimed right, the ball will go over the heads of the infield, especially if they have come in a little expecting another bunt.

Of course, if you miss, you will have a strike called against you, and it's best to give up the idea of bunting. The infield is wise to you. In fact, they may try to trick you into believing that they are expecting the bunt. Then someone will be ready to cover any position that opens as a result of their running in on the bunt.

Baserunning

The rules for baserunning are the same for both fast-pitch and slow-pitch games, except that in slow-pitch a batter is not allowed to bunt the ball, nor is she allowed to steal a base.

In order for a batter to become a base runner, she either has to hit the ball into fair territory or be hit by a pitched ball. Also, should the catcher drop the third strike, when no one is on base or at any time when there are two outs, the batter can advance to first base, just as in baseball.

Two base runners may not occupy the same base. The right to a base is given to a runner who first occupies it. She holds that base until she has touched the next base or until she is forced to leave that base for the next runner.

A base runner is allowed to advance to another base without being declared out under the following conditions: when a fielder gets into the base runner's path or when she is forced to leave a base because the batter was awarded that base—as, for example, when the batter is walked.

Once you've hit the ball, you've got to reach first base safely. From there, you'll try to move to second and third, and hopefully score a run. Many games are decided by only one run, so winning may rest on your ability to successfully run bases.

As you hit the ball, your weight is on the forward foot. This leg holds your weight as you push off to begin running. The first movement toward first base is with the rear foot. Don't add an extra step by shifting your weight to the rear and taking the first step with the forward leg. One extra step may mean a delay that could cause an out.

Don't break your stride to watch the ball. Glance quickly over your shoulder if the ball is behind you, but otherwise your eyes are fixed on the target—first base.

Tag the base on the foul line side with either foot. Don't try to come to an immediate halt, or you'll fall. Also, you are allowed to overrun first base. If you do overrun it, turn right after slowing down. If you turn left, they will think you are trying to advance to second base and you may be tagged out before you get back to first.

If you hit a double, you may go to second base, but you are not allowed to overrun it. As you near first base, curve a bit toward the right. You can do that by leaning to the right and taking a few steps away from the foul line. Touch the inside corner of the bag without breaking your stride. As you gain experience in baserunning, you will learn to touch the bag with your left foot and cross the right foot over as you aim for the next base. Don't expect to be perfect quickly. Practice this until you don't trip over your own feet.

Even as you advance toward second base, be ready to stop suddenly and return to first if the ball has been caught on the fly or has been thrown back to the infield. Trying to stretch a single

The runner is out. She may have wasted time watching the hit ball or perhaps wasted steps when she began her sprint to first base.

into a double could be the reason why the ball was thrown quickly back to the infield.

Sliding

If there isn't too much time to get back to first, the rules permit you to slide. A slide in girls' softball has caused a minor controversy. Some people claim that sliding for girls is dangerous. However, if the player is dressed with full protection, there is no reason to avoid a slide. Besides, a slide gives you two advantages over an upright base runner. You can stop running quickly without a decrease in speed before the slide. Also, a sliding player

The straight-in slide.

The bent-leg slide.

makes a smaller target for the baseperson to tag out.

There are three kinds of slides: the straight-in, the bent-leg, and the hook slide.

Begin the *straight-in* slide about nine or ten feet from the base. Prepare to slide along the ground by allowing the body to lean away from the plate while you are moving forward, toward it. Then throw your weight on one leg and fall while still running. You will slide along the dirt into the plate. If you are wearing spikes, bend the sliding leg at the knee so the spikes will not catch. The other leg and your arms should not touch the ground.

The hook slide is used to avoid being tagged by the first baseperson.

If you want to slide into a base, but want to be able to get up quickly and run toward the next base, you use the *bent-leg* slide. This maneuver begins like the straight-in slide but you slide in much closer to the bag. As you slide, the free leg is bent at the knee, ready for action, but not yet touching the ground. You don't fall backward and away from the plate as hard as you do in the straight-in slide. When the skidding leg tags the bag, prepare to stand up. To do so, bring your weight forward by pushing your arms ahead. Your weight is shifted to the top of the bent leg. Your first running step as you come to your feet will be on the sliding leg which now has not weight on it.

The *hook* slide is a straight-in slide, but more directly into the bag. As you slide in, hook your right foot at the corner and hold your hands and elbows up and out of the way. Leave the ground with your left foot, lean back, and shift your weight to the left side.

A runner must not leave the bag until the ball leaves the pitcher's hand. Stand with your left foot against the base with the right leg aimed for the next one. Your legs are bent at the knees, your arms hanging by your side, and your weight forward. As soon as the ball is released by the pitcher, start running, but be careful. If it's a fly ball or a strike, you will need to return to the base.

Stealing

While you're on base, keep your eye on the pitcher until she puts her foot in contact with the pitcher's plate. She has to step backward off the plate, if she's going to try to pick you off base. This might encourage you to try to steal a base (it is allowed in fast-pitch softball), but if you do begin to run, it is the catcher who will throw you out, not the pitcher. If the game is almost over and an out against your team would mean a loss, then you would be wise to play it safe.

The proper position for a base runner.

The runner should leave the base after the ball leaves the pitcher's hand.

Before you decide whether or not to steal, there are several things to think about: the inning, the score, the skill of your opponents, and the skill of the next batter. Don't forget that the pitcher is also thinking hard about what you might do. She may purposely mislead you into thinking that she is not aware of your actions. So, at times, you may have to out-think the other players. When your team is on the field, you will have to place yourself in the position of the base runner in order to anticipate her next move.

There is a clever, but risky, maneuver called *delayed steal*. In thinking of this action, you must be completely honest with yourself. Are you one of the fastest runners on your team? Can you travel the distance between the bases in three seconds or less? If not, leave the delayed steal for the fast runners.

There should be no more than one out against your team when doing this maneuver. The time to start is when you are on first base and a teammate is on third. The delayed steal can force the catcher into a tough decision as to where to throw the ball. Her hesitation may allow one or more runners to move up. Here is the strategy.

While the catcher holds the ball, take the usual lead from first base, but don't go too far. The catcher may throw the ball to first, forcing you back or even out if you can't get back in time. Also, you may give away your plan by taking too big a lead. But if you have not alarmed the catcher, she will get ready to throw the ball to the pitcher so the game may continue. As soon as you see this, take off as quickly as possible for second base.

The catcher may pause, wondering what to do. About halfway to second, slow down slightly. This can cause even more problems for the catcher. If she throws to second base, you may have time to either reach the base or return to first. Also, while the catcher and second baseperson concentrate on you, the runner on third might break for home. The catcher may send the ball to the third baseperson, which will leave you open to continue on to second base.

However, there are dangers in carrying out a two-person delayed steal. If you, the runner on first, are not as fast as you think, you may get caught in a rundown between first and second. Even worse, you may get tagged out, and the runner heading for home might get trapped and put out. If your team already has one out, then these two outs would retire the side. Certainly, the delayed steal involves a large gamble that should not be taken lightly.

See Chapter 6 for more advanced offensive skills.

Chapter 5.

Pitching and Catching: The Basic Defensive Skills

If you're playing softball in a vacant lot for fun, you will probably switch from position to position in the field. This is a good idea because not only will you get the feel of various positions, it will help you decide which is your best spot. Then, if you begin playing with an organized team, you will probably be assigned to your favorite position once you tell the coach of your experience.

The descriptions of positions which follow apply equally to slow-pitch and fast-pitch softball, with some exceptions which are noted.

Pitching

In softball, the pitching motion is underhand, so to be a pitcher, you must have outstanding ability to throw the ball that way. Three characteristics mark a good pitcher: speed, a variety of pitches, and accuracy. It is the last one which is most important, for it alone applies to all the forms of softball. A pitcher must be able to throw the ball exactly where she wants it to go.

The fast-pitch pitcher needs more variety in the types of pitches she throws than any other pitcher, but the pitcher in a slow-pitch game has to be a better fielder and fast in moving about. She has to jump back when the ball is hit right at her. She has to chase after infield hits, grounders, and little rolling balls.

Speed, versatility, and accuracy can come only with much practice and patience. The successful pitcher spends long hours throwing a softball at a target painted on a garage wall or on a cardboard suspended from a rope. She will not quit until she can send the ball exactly where she wants it to go, time after time. (*See also* Chapter 7.)

Catching

Being a catcher is a tough job, too, and the girl behind home plate is actually the defensive leader of the team. She must be alert, have the ability to react quickly to any situation in the game, and be able to move quickly and easily. She should also have a high degree of accuracy with her throws. A strong arm is not essential, but pinpoint accuracy is a must. In the fast-pitch game, the catcher is often the first to reach a bunted ball and fire it to the first baseperson. Sloppy throwing will ruin the play.

Consider all the other jobs that a good catcher handles. She advises the pitcher about the kind of pitches to throw. She must be ready to spring and catch a pop-up or scramble for a bunt. In fact, she is the first to spot a potential bunt situation.

Of course, in the more popular slow-pitch game, the catcher does not have to worry about base stealing or bunting. Instead, she concentrates on studying a batter's style to try to spot her opponents' weaknesses. She must be strong and brave enough to block home plate and stop a run from scoring.

Playing First Base

The three abilities most necessary in a first baseperson are

The catcher.

quick reactions, nimble footwork, and accuracy in both short and long throws. The need for fast reactions comes from the fact that the first baseperson must be ready to move in to scoop up a grounder or grab a short line drive and then zing the ball to second or third base, almost in one motion. She has to be fast!

Playing Second Base

Some of the same qualities are needed by the second baseperson. She must be able to move easily and throw the ball quickly and accurately. The second quality is a must when executing a double play—a maneuver in which she is often involved

The first baseperson.

The second baseperson is standing on base, waiting for the ball so she can tag out the runner.

with the shortstop. Since most of her throws are usually to first or third base, she does not need the long-distance throwing ability.

Playing Third Base

The ability to make split-second decisions is also needed by the third baseperson. For example, she may be playing in, expecting a low grounder. Suddenly a powerful line drive comes her way. If she doesn't react quickly enough, she'll be hit by the ball.

The third baseperson stays a short distance from her base which is in the lower lefthand corner of the photo.

Playing Shortstop

Versatility, the ability to do many things well, is the best word to describe a shortstop. This player is stationed halfway between second and third base. If you prefer this position, you must be fast, agile, and able to throw a ball accurately while possibly being off-balance.

A shortstop does not stand around waiting for a ball. She is constantly charging in or acting like an outfielder. Should a pop

fly not be deep enough for an outfielder, she must quickly decide where the ball will land and run to that spot. At times, she must backpedal, and that can be difficult. Not only can she lose speed, but there's always the chance of tripping.

Experienced players look upon the shortstop position as a combination of second baseperson, third baseperson, outfielder, and shortstop. This is true only in a fast-pitch game, where there is no shortfielder.

Playing the Outfield

No matter which outfield position you play, you will need two skills to be a success: catching and throwing the ball. Perhaps the single most important technique is how to catch a ball. Whether the ball is a grounder, or a fly ball, or a ball thrown by another player, there are standard procedures common to all three.

Whether you're playing right, center, or left field, the outfielder is more active in softball, especially slow-pitch softball, than in baseball. The two qualities needed most for the outfielder are quickness and a strong, accurate throwing arm. The center fielder has to be the fastest of all three. Also, she should have the most powerful throwing arm. The center fielder covers more territory than the other two outfielders. That is because the playing areas of both left and right field are smaller, due to the foul line running through them.

The outfielder runs in to catch the ball.

Shortfield

The shortfielder is a tenth position, used only in the slow-pitch game. She has to be very fast and have the qualities of both the shortstop and an outfielder.

In most games, the shortfielder is a "rover"—she is all over the field, from deep in the outfield to near the base lines. (For a fuller discussion of this position, see Chapter 7.)

An outfielder also needs sharp judgment. For example, you have to keep in mind the wind and how that can influence the path and speed of a fly ball. You have to note the runners on base and where they will advance. You must know how many outs there are and what inning it is. All these factors will affect the catch and help determine to which person you will throw the ball.

As you wait for the ball, be sure your feet are firmly and comfortably placed on the ground. Your weight should be· distributed on the balls of both feet. Knees are slightly bent.

An important rule to remember: *never take your eye off the ball*. You will have to judge where the ball will land and shift your position accordingly. If you are an infield player, and the ball is hit to the right or left near you, move diagonally toward it. The reverse occurs when the ball is hit deeply to your right or left. Now you will move diagonally backward.

Deciding how fast you move and exactly where the ball will land depend upon how far the ball is hit, its speed, and its angle of flight. Experience will help you estimate where the ball will land without constantly running back and forth. Practice sessions with a friend batting a ball to you will sharpen your ability to make quick decisions.

Keeping her eye on the ball.

As you watch the ball approach, decide if it is going to reach you above or below the waist. The placement of the ball will determine your catching strategy. Should the ball come to you above the waist, place your hands together so the thumbs are

To catch a ball above the waist, raise both hands together.

touching. Your fingers' point upward. However, if the ball is below the waist, set your hands together so the little fingers make contact. Your fingers now point downward. By using these techniques, you will allow yourself more space for moving your arm

As the ball smacks the glove, trap it in place by covering it with your throwing hand.

up, down, or sideways. They will also help eliminate the possibility that the ball will slam straight down on your fingertips.

Now, as the ball smacks the glove or mitt, trap it in place by covering it with your throwing hand. At the same time, use the

When the approaching ball is below the waist, place both hands down with fingers pointing to the ground.

throwing hand to bring the ball back toward your body to prevent it from bouncing away. This keeps you from making extra movements before immediately sending the ball on its way again.

As the ball strikes the glove, pull back a little but cover the ball with the other hand quickly.

Now that you have the basic catching skills, there are some special ways to catch a ball. These depend upon the type of ball that is to be caught.

For example, the hitter sends a *ground ball* in your direction. This can be tricky, because the playing field can be rough and cause unexpected bounces. Therefore, you may have difficulty judging where to catch the ball. Keep your eye on it. Do not move backward. That will allow the ball to "play you," rather than you playing the ball. In other words, you will be chasing after the ball, losing precious time. Shift your weight foward and run toward it in a low position so you don't have to bend over when you reach the ball.

Once in place, with the ball coming at you, spread your feet comfortably with the left foot slightly ahead of the right. Bend your knees and hips so that your glove touches the ground. Do not let the ball roll under your glove. You want to catch that grounder just after it begins the last bounce. However, it very often happens that the last bounce sends the ball into the air. Then you will have to switch and use the technique for catching a ball above the waist.

When fielding a grounder hit directly at you or to the left, try to catch the ball inside your left foot. Should the ball be coming from the right, stop the ball inside the right foot.

As soon as the ball strikes the glove, let your hands give a little and cover it with your throwing hand. One mistake that some beginners make when catching a grounder is looking away too soon. Keep your eye on the ball until you are sure it's firmly in your glove or mitt. Then glance at the base or at the girl to whom you will be throwing the ball, and make your play.

Use these same techniques when catching a *thrown ball*. Unlike grounders, most thrown balls arrive above the waist.

There is an additional difference between catching a grounder and a thrown ball. With a grounder, you move in and are ready ahead of time. Usually with a thrown ball, you hope to tag out the base runner who may have lost sight of the ball. You do not want to give away the fact that you are about to receive the ball or she may put on an unexpected burst of speed and reach the base safely. As always, keep your eyes on the ball, but do not raise your hands into position until the last moment.

Just as the starter gun begins a footrace, the crack of a bat is your signal to begin catching a *fly ball*. You move immediately so that you can be in place before the ball comes down. Even as you run, you are judging the height, speed, and wind effect of the fly ball. If the ball is hit high, this will give you a few extra seconds to get into position. But if a strong wind is blowing, be ready to adjust for it.

If you decide the ball is going to land a short distance behind you, turn and move sideways and backward to that spot. At all times, keep a watch on that fly ball. It is unwise to turn your back on a long fly ball until you are certain that you will need some time to get back far enough to catch it. Even then, try to look at the ball as you run. It is better to be a few steps back from where you think the ball will land. Always be prepared for the ball to drop suddenly in a stiff breeze or to sail on beyond where you thought it might land. A fielder can easily move up a few steps to grab the ball, but moving backward is tricky and slower. Also, there is a chance that you might stumble.

Once you are in position and watching the ball come down, keep your legs spread comfortably and your left leg slightly forward. This will put you in a position to throw the ball immediately upon catching it. As with other above-the-waist catches, raise your hands, thumbs together, and upon impact,

In throwing the ball, most softball players prefer to hold it with the thumb and first two fingers. The other fingers are spaced comfortably around the ball.

pull in your arms a little and cover the ball to prevent losing it. Your fingers of the throwing hand should be curled about the ball as you cover it so that you can snap it to a teammate.

Throwing the ball is the second skill a defensive player must continually try to improve. The first step to successful throwing is your grip, which is determined by hand size. If your hand is small, hold the ball between the thumb and first two fingers. Your third and fourth fingers are spaced around it and, if possible, stretched out so that you will have a firmer grasp on the softball. If your hands are larger, the thumb and first two fingers are in the same location, but your third and fourth fingers will reach much farther around the ball. Comfort and control of the ball are the most important factors. If you can, have your fingers cross the seams of the ball. This will prevent the ball from slipping when you release it during the throw.

Be sure only the fleshy tips of your fingers are gripping the ball. No other part of your hand or palm should touch it. A good test to judge if you are holding the ball correctly is to see if daylight shows between the ball and your hand. If not, you are holding the ball with too much of that hand. This may interfere with the speed of the throw and its accuracy.

Once you have a good grasp on the ball, you move into the second stage of throwing. Shift your weight to your back leg. Then, move your front foot forward and bring the throwing arm far behind your body. If you are not certain that your arm has gone back far enough, keep reaching back until you can feel a pull in your elbow. To add distance to your throw, your hand should be bent at the wrist.

Now you are ready to whip the ball forward. Shift your weight forward onto the front leg and pivot your body so you are almost facing where the ball is to go. Practice the throwing action in

Some players use the five-finger grip that has the five fingers spread evenly around the whole softball.

slow motion a few times so you can follow the next steps in the correct order. The whipping of the ball begins with your shoulder. Then, when your elbow is above your shoulder, your forearm moves ahead. As your hand points at the target, release the ball with a snap of the wrist.

Even though the ball is now in the air, your throw is not completed. You want to "follow-through." This may seem needless because you no longer have the ball, but players who try to stop the follow-through too soon limit the strength and aim in their throw. So, once the ball is released, keep moving your hand. Your rear leg will almost move automatically forward to about shoulder distance from your other foot.

There are slight variations on this basic throwing technique, depending on whether the throw is short or long. If the throw is a short one, you hold onto the ball a bit longer. Or, for example, if you are deep into the outfield and want to reach the third baseperson, release the ball quickly. This will cause the ball to arc higher. If the throw is really a long one, say to home plate, aim the ball so it lands about ten feet in front of the girl handling that position. She will catch the ball on the first bounce.

Estimating when to release the ball comes with practice. Have a friend join you for a session on a large field where you can keep changing the distances separating you. As you throw the ball at different lengths, keep the rule in mind. The farther the ball has to go, the sooner you let it go.

When you have mastered the techniques for throwing a softball, work to perfect the four basic throws: the underhand toss, the sidearm throw, the overhand throw, and the overhand snap.

The *underhand toss* is used for quick, short throws. Bring your arm back and straighten your upper arm and forearm. Angle the wrist so the hand points up. As you start your throwing motion,

the upper arm remains pointed downward, but the forearm sweeps forward. Then, the upper arm moves forward as you release the ball. You can get the distance you want by whipping the forearm and wrist at the moment you release the ball.

A *sidearm throw* will come in handy if you are playing the infield. Extend your arm diagonally out and down from the shoulder. Then bend your forearm up at the elbow. As you swing your whole arm forward, lower your forearm so it is parallel to the ground. Release the ball and follow through by swinging your arm across your body.

The *overhand throw* is a basic one for all players, and the only one used by an outfielder. This type of throw gives the ball speed and distance.

To begin the overhand throw, raise your forearm above your head with your wrist bent back. Then swing your arm forward and down in the follow through.

An *overhand snap* is similar to the overhand throw. This maneuver is used mainly by a catcher and occasionally by infielders. The purpose is to speed the ball toward its destination with the least time loss. All you do is actually shorten the overhand throw by firing the ball as your hand reaches ear level. In order to gain distance and speed for the ball, the wrist must snap quickly.

Keep practicing these four basic throws until they become part of you. You don't say to yourself, "Oh, I must use the overhand snap." You see what has to be done and then do it.

Use the underhand throw for quick, short throws.

The sidearm throw is good for playing the infield.

The overhand throw gives the ball speed and distance.

Most thrown balls arrive above the waist.

Chapter 6.

Getting Better and Better: Advanced Hitting and Running

Certain skills that relate to batting and baserunning can make you a better offensive player. Because players use these advanced techniques, teams are able to win games.

Place Hitting

When you first began playing softball, you were hoping just to *hit* the ball. Once you started hitting well, you saw situations during a game when it would have helped if you could hit the ball right where you *wanted* it to go. Often a batter can spot holes in the field—places where the defensive players might have a hard time reaching in order to stop or catch the ball.

In general, grip alone can help you aim a batted ball. For example, if you want to hit a long fly because the outfielders are playing in, use the long grip on the bat. Your swing will need as much power as you can gather, so swing slightly upward, and the follow-through will send the ball high.

Another time to change your grip is when you're facing a fastball pitcher. Use a choke grip on the bat. It will give you a faster swing. The ball won't go as far, but your accuracy will be improved.

Other place-hitting techniques depend on when and where you hit the ball. Generally, you have three possible landing sites: right, center, and left field.

Suppose you want the ball to land in right field. Where the ball actually lands will depend on where in the swing the bat and ball make contact. If you are a righty batter, try to hit the ball

Place hitting is an important skill. This batter hit a flyball to the outfield. It will either give her time to reach first or she will be out if the ball is caught. She might have been wiser to hit a line drive to left field.

when it has arrived at just beyond the center of your body and is about to pass by you on its way to the catcher. If you want the ball to land in center field, make contact when the ball has not yet reached the center of your body. For a hit to left field, you want to make contact when the ball has reached the exact center of your body. Snap your wrists sharply so that the ball is pulled to the left.

A batter who hits lefty will have to reverse the above suggestions, except for hitting into center field.

Hit-and-Run

When you are able to place a ball where you want, you can use that skill in a hit-and-run play. This occurs when there is a runner on first base. Not only does she want to get to second, but you, the batter, need to reach first without causing an out. Teamwork is required.

As soon as the ball leaves the pitcher's hand, the girl on first base speeds toward second. The baseperson there spots this and moves in to cover the base. There is now a hole in the infield, and that's where you want to send the ball. But there's a danger with a hit-and-run. Your sharp line drive into the hole may head right to a fielder. If she gets to the ball quickly, there's the strong possibility of at least one out and possibly a double play.

Chapter 7.

Tightening Up the Defense: Advanced Pitching, Catching, and Throwing

To increase or add to the basic defensive skills discussed in Chapter 5, each player can learn new plays that will help her to become more expert at her position.

Being the team's pitcher means that you have a special talent or skill that none of the other players have. Although each pitcher uses similar types of delivery and pitches, each one has developed those techniques into her own style.

A variety of wind-ups and deliveries is available. A wind-up has two purposes: to keep the batter guessing and to gain full power for the pitch. Three kinds of pitches will achieve those goals: windmill, slingshot, and figure-eight.

The *windmill* delivery got its name because the pitcher makes a full sweep with her arm before hurling the ball. Begin as you would all deliveries, with the hands gripping the ball at waist level. Shift your weight to the foot on the pitching arm side. As you raise the pitching hand over your head, start moving the other foot forward to keep your balance. Your arm continues to swing all the way around and the foot on the non-pitching side completes its move ahead. Footwork and the muscle strength in the arm combine to give force to the pitch.

Because your arm has moved so quickly through such a wide arc, the pitched ball will have tremendous speed. Unfortunately, the accuracy of the windmill pitch is hard to predict.

More accuracy can be obtained with the *slingshot* delivery. This action produces a straight, fast pitch which has force plus control. Remember that in slow-pitch softball, the umpire will regulate the speed of all pitches.

Grip the ball so that your hand is securely around the ball. Be sure your fingertips cross the seams so that when pitched, the ball will twist as much as you want it to. As you begin the wind-up, both feet touch the pitcher's plate if the game is a fast-pitch one. In slow-pitch, the pitcher may touch the plate with only one foot before beginning the wind-up.

The slingshot is a simple back-and-forth motion of the pitching arm. The hand holding the ball swings way, way back, higher than the shoulder. Then as you step forward, you come down with the ball, releasing it with a wrist snap just as your hand gets beyond your thigh.

A combination of the windmill and slingshot deliveries is the *figure-eight*. Bring the pitching arm back, away from your body, as far as possible. Then sweep the arm around and release the ball, snapping the wrist. This gives a whiplike motion which speeds the ball on its way.

The basic starting position to pitch a ball. From this position, the pitcher could slip into the windmill, slingshot, or figure-eight delivery.

For the slingshot, bring your arm back as far as you can.

Then step forward, swinging your arm forward and snapping your wrist.

The thrown ball will have speed, but due to the odd arm movements, the control over the pitch may be weak. This delivery is the most difficult of the three basic pitches and should be attempted only after much practice.

Of the three kinds of deliveries, beginners should perfect the slingshot style first. In fact, many softball pitchers, once they have mastered that delivery, prefer not to use the other two at all.

Do not use a wind-up for greatest speed in the slow-pitch game. The umpire may warn you once, but if you pitch the ball too fast again, you may be sent to the showers. In slow-pitch, the idea is control, not speed, as far as pitchers are concerned.

In the fast-pitch game, most pitchers prefer the *drop-pitch* because the ball has great speed. Just when the batter thinks she has a fix on the ball, it sinks very suddenly. A drop-pitch is almost impossible to hit.

The drop-pitch grip.

Hold the ball very tightly, with fingers across the seams. Use the two-finger grip, which means the forefinger and middle finger are over the ball with the other fingers on each side and the bottom. If possible, have those two fingers across the seams. Release the ball from your fingertips. Some pitchers pull their hand up at the last moment to give the ball a bit more spin, but generally, simply releasing the ball in an underhand motion will give it enough spin.

The *rise-pitch* behaves in the opposite manner. As the ball

The rise-pitch grip.

approaches the batter at waist level, it suddenly "takes off," or rises to the chin level as it crosses the plate.

The secret of the rise-pitch is in the grip. The pitcher holds the ball with her hand practically sideways. The middle and index fingers are slightly off center with the thumb on one side and the other fingers bent along the other side. The middle finger is arched, bending at the second and third joints. The middle of the arch does not touch the ball. As you release the pitch, force your index finger up and to the left. This will spin the ball counterclockwise.

The *knuckle ball* is a slow ball, but it is unpredictable and very difficult for a batter to hit. Unfortunately, such a pitch is also hard for a catcher to grab if the batter does not hit the ball. For this reason, a knuckle ball is never used when runners are on base or if the score is tight. The catcher's fumble would probably allow a runner to steal the next base. Also, the flight of a knuckle ball is so slow that, again, a base runner might advance another base. However, under the right conditions, this type of pitch can disturb the batter's concentration.

The grip for a knuckle ball is totally different than for other pitches. Your thumb and pinky should be at each side of the ball. The three middle fingers are bent with the knuckles pressing against the ball. A variation is to dig your three fingertips into the ball, which allows the ball to float without spinning. The fingers act like claws.

To release the ball, the thumb and little fingers merely let go. The ball then seems to float toward the batter. In fact, the knuckle pitch is the slowest moving ball in the game. As a result, the throw has been dubbed the "change-of-pace" pitch. It is popular in slow-pitch softball.

The *curve* ball has a second name, too: the *wasted pitch*.

When the pitcher releases the ball in a certain manner, the ball will curve toward the batter. This action causes the ball to purposely miss the strike zone.

Why would a pitcher use such a ball?

A curve ball can occasionally catch a batter unaware. She has been accustomed to the ball either dipping or rising, and suddenly here comes a ball that does neither. The batter might be over-anxious and swing, for a strike.

Gripping a curve ball is the same as for a regular, fast pitch. The difference comes at the moment of release. Snap your wrist either to the left or to the right. The ball rolls off the inside or the outside of your hand, curving in the direction in which you snapped your wrist.

Catcher

In slow-pitch softball, the catcher has it a lot easier than in fast-pitch. The reason for this is that she does not have to worry about base stealing or bunting and she is not required to wear the body protector or the mask. The pitcher and catcher must be able to work as a close combination. The catcher guides a pitcher to the exact sort of pitch to throw. If the pitcher becomes upset, the catcher is the person who walks out to the mound to calm her down so that she'll regain control.

Although many girls would be excellent catchers, they never go out for that position. The reason is a fear of the bat. Because the catcher is behind the plate, there is always danger from the batter. Beginners often sling the bat after they hit a ball, unaware of where it will be flying. Catchers should know who these "bat throwers" are and be very careful when one enters the batter's box. Otherwise, unless the catcher moves in too close, the number of bat injuries is small.

How does a catcher go about her job?

Wearing her protective equipment, the catcher squats behind the batter's box. She bends the ankles, knees, and hips so that her body is as low as possible. Her weight should rest on her toes with the knees comfortably spread.

In slow-pitch, there is no set way to position the catcher. She can squat, crouch low on both legs or on one leg, or even stand on one side of the plate and lean over.

Using prearranged signals, the catcher communicates with the pitcher by placing the fingers of her throwing hand against the inside of her thigh. Usually, the right leg is used. Care must be taken not to let members of the opposing team detect these signals. Once the pitcher has either accepted the signs or requested another type of pitch, the catcher then provides a target for the pitcher by raising her mitt into position. She protects the fingers of her throwing hand by clenching them into a loose fist.

As the ball leaves the pitcher's hand, she rises to a semi-standing position with her feet solidly spaced. This position gives her more freedom to catch the ball and throw it to either the pitcher or the baseperson. If she's wearing a mask, she should flip it off whenever she fields a ball or has a backup play.

Infield Positions

A first baseperson is always set to put a runner out. In slow-pitch, since bunting is not allowed, she can play even with the bag or a few feet behind it. In fast-pitch, she has to move in, ready for a bunt. She does not need a great deal of strength in her arm, but she should know how to stretch her body.

If you're playing first, should the ball come straight at you, step toward the ball with your mitt-side leg and touch the base

A catcher signalling the pitcher.

The first baseperson steps toward the coming ball.

with the opposite foot. Save time by reaching out for the ball. However, if a ball approaches you wide on the mitt side, step in that direction, keeping the opposite foot on the base. When a ball is far to the non-mitt side, reach over and grab the ball, tapping the base with the foot opposite your mitt side.

Should the catcher fire the ball to you in an attempted pick-off play to put out a runner, straddle the base and swing the upper portion of your body toward the ball. When you catch the ball, tag the base with your mitt.

As difficult as it is to be a first baseperson, many experienced ballplayers recognize the *second baseperson* as the most challenging of the three positions to play. She plays to the right side of the bag along the base line. She has to be good at "pivoting." That means she has to turn in place, without taking extra steps. She has to make those double-play throws. She catches the ball, tags the base, turns, gets out of the way of any runner, and makes her throw to first very fast. Perfecting a double play is a must for the second baseperson. Her worst enemy is a runner, who may slam into her.

The important thing to do is to time the run so that she catches the ball as she steps onto the bag with her right foot. When she's got the ball, she should advance a step with the same foot so that she is beyond the base, then pivot on the right leg, move a step forward with the left, and throw the ball to first base.

The second baseperson in a slow-pitch game needs skill in running after fly balls and in scooping up ground balls. Also, as in fast-pitch, she has to be super in making double plays.

The *shortstop* can also be the pivot person for a double play. She will generally run directly to second base which she tags with her left foot as she catches the ball. She advances a step with the right foot, another step with the left foot, and throws to first base.

In slow-pitch ball, the shortstop has to be able to get rid of the ball in a hurry. She must have excellent speed and great fielding ability. In fact, a shortstop in both types of games needs to be great in all defensive areas, including fast reflexes.

The *shortfielder* of the slow-pitch game was added because slow-pitch softball is a hitter's game. The action is fast and often. There is no boredom in the outfield during a slow-pitch game.

Although the shortfielder plays anywhere in the outfield, she must study the batters more than the other outfielders. She has to know where certain hitters like to hit the ball and try to be where the ball lands. Her usual place, however, is to the left of second base if the batter is right-handed and to the right if the batter is left-handed. She plays shallow outfield and is often as busy as a shortstop. Her skills are those of a shortstop, but she needs a stronger arm for those long throws to the plate.

Chapter 8.

Health and Diet

Maintaining a good diet will help any softball player. Stick to a high-protein, low-calorie menu such as meat, eggs, and cheese.

An excellent means of keeping in condition is to go out for other sports. Fortunately, most people who enjoy playing softball also take part in volleyball, bowling, or tennis. Running, a form of exercise which has hit high national interest in the last few years, will also help to keep you in good shape.

No player should enter a game "cold," without proper loosening-up. You won't be able to play at your best and you will run the risk of pulled or strained muscles as well as other injuries. The cooler the temperature, the longer the workout should be before taking your place on the field. There are special exercises you can do.

To improve your arm and shoulder strength, try this exercise. Extend your arms out at right angles to your body. Circle them eight times in one direction and then reverse the circles for eight more times. Do each set of 16 circles four times.

Still another way to build your arms is by doing pushups. Keep working at them until you can do about 50 at one stretch.

An excellent way to develop arm power as well as improve your throwing ability is to hurl a heavier ball than usual back and forth with another person, several times a day. You can make your own heavy ball by adding weight to a softball. Soak it in water or wrap it with thick tape.

These exercises will help to warm up the leg muscles and prevent injury.

Most players can limber up by running at a moderate speed once or twice around the diamond or a similar distance. They should also do some calisthenics—mostly stretching exercises. Try some deep knee bends and a few moments of running in place.

Another good limbering up exercise begins with spreading your feet apart. Without bending your knees, touch your right foot with your left hand and then your left foot with your right hand. If you're doing this properly, you can feel the muscles that you want to use while playing getting a workout. The muscles behind the leg and thigh—the hamstring muscles—show the effects of exercise quickly. The most common leg injury in softball is a pulled hamstring muscle. Many of these injuries could be prevented with a warming-up period before a game.

There are two more exercises which will help those same muscles as well as loosen up your body in general. Lie on your back. Lift your right leg up so that it is perpendicular to the ground. Clasp your hands under the thigh just above the knee and pull toward your head. Lower that leg and do the same with your left leg.

Stand with your feet spread apart. Shift your left leg far to the left. Placing your right hand on the right hip and letting the left arm dangle, push your weight as far to the left as possible. You should be able to feel the muscles in your right leg stretching. Now reverse legs and do the same. This will permit the muscles in the left leg to benefit.

Common Softball Terms and Phrases

You will notice that most softball terms and phrases have come directly from baseball. Some of them seem to have little connection with the true meaning of the words. Often their origin has been lost over the years.

ALTERED BAT: One on which an illegal physical change has been done. For example, a metal bat which has the metal handle replaced by a wooden handle would be considered an altered bat.

APPEAL PLAY: One on which an umpire cannot make a decision until requested by a player or coach. This appeal must be made before the next pitch, legal or illegal. An example of an appeal play might be when a person bats out of order or does not touch a base.

ASSIST: A fielding credit that goes to a player who helped another make a put-out.

AWAY: The number of outs. "One away" means one out.

BACKSTOP: A name given to the fence behind home plate; another name for the catcher.

BAG: The base

BALK: A pitcher commits a balk when she makes a motion to pitch a ball but does not deliver immediately. When a balk is called, the batter is given a ball and the base runners are permitted to advance one base.

BASE ON BALLS: When four balls are called on a batter, she may advance to first base without being put out.

BASE PATH: An imaginary line on the playing field. This path extends three feet to either side of a direct line between the bases.

BASE RUNNER: A player who is on any base.

BASES FULL: *See* Bases Loaded.

BASES LOADED: A runner is on each base.

BATTED BALL: Any ball that is hit by the bat or hits the bat and lands either in fair or foul territory. No intention to hit the ball is necessary for one to qualify as a batted ball.

BATTER-BASE RUNNER: This player has finished her turn at bat but has not yet touched first base or been put out at first base.

BATTER'S BOX: The area where the batter must stand while in position to hit balls pitched by the opposing team's pitcher.

BATTERY: The name given to the pitcher and the catcher of a team. The term originated because the pitcher and catcher are considered the source of power for a team.

BATTING AVERAGE: Divide the total number of hits a batter has achieved by the total number of times she has been at bat.

BATTING ORDER: The official order in which a team must come to bat.

BEAN BALL: A ball pitched too close to the batter's head.

BEAT OUT: To either bunt or hit a slowly moving ball and arrive at first base safely.

BEHIND ON THE COUNT: Either the batter or the pitcher

may be "behind on the count." A batter is when she has more strikes than balls. The reverse is true when the pitcher is behind on the count.

BLOCKED BALL: A batted or thrown ball which is interfered with by someone not officially connected with the game. A blocked ball also occurs when a ball touches any object that is not part of the official playing area or equipment. It automatically becomes a dead ball. *See also* Dead Ball.

BLOOPER: A batted ball which arcs over the heads of the infielders and lands in shallow outfield making it difficult for anyone to reach.

BOBBLE: Fumbling with the ball while attempting to make a catch.

BOX: The areas of the batter, catcher, and coaches.

BOX SCORE: Total number of runs, hits, and errors in a game.

BUNT: A legally hit ball that is not swung at but is tapped slowly within the infield.

CALLING SIGNALS: The kinds of pitches called for by the catcher. This is not actually called out but given to the pitcher using a system of secret signals.

CATCH: A batted or thrown ball that is stopped when the

fielder catches the ball with her hands or glove or mitt. The ball must be held in the player's hands or glove and not by an article of clothing or other portion of her body. Should the player drop the ball while she attempts to throw it, the catch is still considered official.

CATCHER'S BOX: The area within which the catcher must stand when calling signals and receiving the pitched ball.

CHANGE OF PACE: Varying the speed of pitches. Generally a change of pace ball is slower than a previous fast pitch. This is designed to upset the batter's timing.

CHARGED CONFERENCE: Any suspension of playing requested by the defensive team during which a representative of that team comes out on the field and meets with her pitcher. The representative must not be a player at the time.

CHOPPED BALL: A ball which the batter purposely chops down with the bat so the ball will bounce very high. It is illegal.

CIRCUIT CLOUT: A home run. The term means the batter has hit, or clouted, the ball so hard that she can make a circuit of all three bases safely.

CLEANUP: The fourth hitter in the batting order. The name stems from the fact that she is usually the best hitter and is able to bring any runners home.

COACH: A member of the team at bat who takes his or her place in the coach's box. He or she will direct the players in running the bases. Two coaches are allowed, one near first base, the other near third.

COUNT: The number of balls and strikes.

CROWD THE PLATE: A batter who stands close to home plate is "crowding the plate."

CUT: To swing at the ball.

DEAD BALL: A ball not in play. This ball will not officially be in play again until the pitcher is within eight feet of the pitcher's plate and the plate umpire has called, "Play ball."

DEFENSIVE TEAM: The team on the field.

DIAMOND: The area formed by home plate and the three bases.

DISLODGED BASE: A base moved from its official position.

DOUBLE PLAY: Two base runners are called out as the result of a batted ball.

DOWN: The number of outs. "Two down" means two outs.

EARNED RUN: A run which was scored as a result of offensive play rather than by an error of the defensive team.

ERROR: A defensive mistake.

FAIR BALL: A batted ball that is stopped or touched in fair territory between home and first base, between home and third base, or which lands in fair territory and does not cross a foul line until after it passes first or third base.

FAIR TERRITORY: Any part of the playing field within and including the first and third base foul lines.

FAN: To strike out.

FIELDER: Any player of the team in the field.

FIELDER'S CHOICE: A play when the fielder puts out a base runner rather than the batter.

FLY BALL: Any ball batted into the air and caught without having touched the ground.

FOOT IN BUCKET: The batter steps away from the plate with her forward foot.

FORCE-OUT: Occurs to avoid two players occupying the same base. For example, when the ball is hit, usually a grounder, the

The catcher should wear protective gear such as a face mask and padding for body and legs. They *must* do so in a fast-pitch game.

113

player on first must run to second to make room for the batter on first, and in so doing is forced at second by the second base-person or shortstop who has touched the base before her.

FOUL BALL: A batted ball outside of fair territory.

FOUL TIP: A batted ball—not higher than the batter's head—which goes directly to the catcher and is caught. This constitutes a strike.

FULL COUNT: Three balls and two strikes.

GRAND SLAM: A home run with the bases loaded. The term comes from the card game of bridge where it means the best a player can get.

GROOVE: The middle of the strike zone.

GROUNDER: A batted ball hit on the ground.

HIT: To make a base hit or to take a turn at bat.

HIT THE DIRT: To slide or to throw yourself safely away from a bean ball.

HOLE: An area in the field not covered by a defensive player.

Waiting her turn at bat, the next hitter is on deck in an area marked off by a white circle. While she waits, she limbers up by swinging the bat.

HOME TEAM: The team on whose ground the game is played. Should the game be played on a neutral field, the home team is determined by the flip of a coin.

ILLEGAL BAT: A bat that does not meet official regulations.

INFIELD: Fair territory that is bounded by and including the base paths.

INFIELD FLY: A fair fly ball that can be caught by an infielder. This occurs when first and second, or first, second and third bases are occupied, but before two are out.

IN FLIGHT: Any batted, thrown, or pitched ball that has not yet touched an object or the ground other than a fielder.

INNING: A division of a softball game where each team has a turn at bat and in which there are three outs for each team.

IN-SHOOT: A curve ball that curves toward the batter.

INSIDE PITCH: A pitched ball which misses the strike zone on the side near the batter.

INTERFERENCE: An act by a defensive player that prevents a batter from hitting a pitched ball or an act by an offensive player which hinders or confuses a defensive player who is attempting to execute a play.

KEYSTONE SACK: Second base.

LAY ONE DOWN. To bunt.

LEAD OFF THE BASE: To move off a base toward the next one before the ball is pitched. This is allowed only in fast-pitch.

LEGAL TOUCH: This happens when a runner is touched by the ball held by a fielder. To be a legal touch, the runner need only be touched with the hand or glove in which the ball is held.

LINE DRIVE: A batted ball that travels in a straight line.

MASK: A device used by the catcher and umpires to protect their faces.

MOVE THE BALL: To hit the ball even though it may be fielded and turned into an out.

OBSTRUCTION: An act by a fielder who hinders a base runner as she is running the bases.

OFFENSIVE TEAM: The team at bat.

ON DECK: The next person to bat. The on deck circle is halfway between the bench and home plate.

OUT: The retirement of a batter or base runner during play.

OUTFIELD: The fair territory on a diamond which is beyond the infield.

OUTSIDE PITCH: A pitched ball which misses the strike zone on the side away from the batter.

OUT-SHOOT: A curve ball that curves away from the batter.

OVERRUN: To run beyond a base.

OVERSLIDE: To slide beyond a base.

OVERTHROW: To throw above the baseperson or fielder's hand.

PASS: A walk.

PASSED BALL: A legally pitched ball which the catcher fails to hold.

PERFECT GAME: One in which the pitcher allowed no hits, no runs, and no player of the opposing team got on base.

PICKOFF: To trap a runner off base.

PICKUP GAME: An informal game not sponsored or organized by any league or organization.

PINCH HITTER: A substitute batter. The term originates from the fact that this person is substituted when the team is losing or in a "pinch."

PITCH OUT: A pitch intentionally thrown wide of the plate so the batter cannot hit the ball.

PIVOT FOOT: The foot which the pitcher must keep in contact with the pitcher's plate until she releases the ball.

PLAY BALL: A term used by the plate umpire to indicate that play shall begin or resume.

POP UP: A short, high fly in or near the infield.

PULL HITTER: A batter who hits the ball too soon and then sharply follows through.

PUTOUT: When a batter hits a fly which is caught as an out; a hitter or base runner who is put out by a thrown ball to a fielder.

QUICK RETURN PITCH: A ball pitched in an attempt to catch the batter off-balance. This pitch is thrown before the batter has assumed the desired position or before she is set after the last pitch.

RBI: Runs batted in.

SACRIFICE and SACRIFICE FLY: Advancing a runner by forcing a play on the batter. A batter hits a sacrifice fly when there are less than two outs so that a runner can score even though that fly ball is caught for an out by the fielder.

SHAKE OFF: A refusal by a pitcher to throw the type of pitch indicated by the catcher. The pitcher communicates this with a negative shake of the head.

SHOESTRING CATCH: A low catch, often diving, by an outfielder. The terms stems from the fact that the fielder appears to be making the catch off her shoestrings.

SHUTOUT: A game in which one team fails to score.

SOUTHPAW: A left-handed batter or pitcher.

SQUEEZE: Bringing a runner home from third by bunting.

STEAL or STEALING: A base runner trying to advance to the next base during a pitch to the batter.

STRAIGHT AWAY: Normal defensive and hitting pattern.

STRIKE ZONE: In fast-pitch, the strike zone is any part of home plate between the batter's armpits and the top of her knees when the batter uses a natural batting stance. In slow-pitch, the strike zone is the space over home plate between the batter's highest shoulder and her knees during a natural batting stance.

TAG: To touch a base with ball in hand before a runner reaches that base or to touch a runner with the ball in hand.

TAG-UP: On a long fly, a runner already on a base, and taking a lead from the base, must go basck to the base, step on it—that is, tag-up—before running toward the next base. She is allowed to run only after the ball has been touched by a fielder. *See also* Lead Off the Base.

TALLY: To score a run.

TEXAS LEAGUER: Weak fly that lands safely.

TIME: A call by the umpire to suspend play.

TRIPLE PLAY: Three outs which are the result of continuous action on one batted ball.

TURN AT BAT: This begins when a player enters the batter's box and ends when she becomes a base runner or is put out.

WALK: This occurs when a batter has four balls called on her. She then advances to first base safely.

WASTE PITCH: A pitch purposely thrown outside the strike zone. This is an attempt to trick the batter into going for a ball she will have difficulty hitting.

WILD PITCH: A legally delivered pitch which the catcher is unable to stop.

INDEX